# Three Little
# Indians

By Gene S. Stuart    Paintings by Louis S. Glanzman

□ BOOKS FOR YOUNG EXPLORERS
NATIONAL GEOGRAPHIC SOCIETY

Many years ago there was an Indian boy named Little Knife.
He lived where the land was flat and covered with grass.
It was a place where the wind often blew.
Winter could bring dark clouds and deep snow.
Little Knife lived with his mother, father, and sister.
They lived together in a buffalo-skin tent called a tepee.
Each family had its own tepee.
The tepees of several families made a village.
These families were part of the Cheyenne people.

Cheyenne children learned to do
grown-up work by playing games.
Girls made toy tepees
and cooked little pots of stew.
Babies spent most of the day
in skin cradles.
A cradle had two stiff, flat boards
on the back.
A mother could stand the cradle
against a tepee or a tree.
Then the baby could watch
as the older children played.

Cheyenne boys wanted to be good buffalo hunters.
They practiced by playing hunting games.
Some of the boys pretended they were buffalo.
A buffalo-boy held a cactus plant to his head
to make believe he had horns.
And he kicked the dust just like a real buffalo.
Other boys were hunters. They moved slowly and made no noise.
The hunters crept close to the buffalo and shot toy arrows.
Then the buffalo-boy fell down and pretended to be dead.

Cheyenne families packed their things
and followed the buffalo, wherever the buffalo moved.
The people needed buffalo meat for food
and the skins for clothes and tepees.
Little Knife would hold the horse steady
while his mother and sister took down the tepee
and packed. Then his mother tied their bundles
on two long poles. When the horse pulled the poles,
the ends dragged on the ground.

Little Knife's father gave him a little pony.
Sometimes Little Knife and his pony raced
across the land as fast as the wind.
Fathers taught their sons to ride so that someday
they could hunt buffalo with the men.

On the day of the buffalo hunt,
the hunters rode their fastest horses.
Little Knife and some other boys followed them
and watched from a hill nearby.
When the hunters came near, the buffalo began to run.
The noise of the buffalo running
was like thunder in a summer storm.
Each hunter rode close beside a buffalo,
and tried to kill it with a bow and arrow or a spear.

9

Every spring all the Cheyenne gathered together.
The men built a house for special meetings.
Some men made music with bone whistles
as they danced around a tall pole.
They took turns and danced
for four days and nights.
The Cheyenne believed this dance
made plants and animals grow.
And they believed the dance
made the people happy.

She-Likes-Somebody was a little Creek girl.
She lived in a village with many houses.
The houses were covered with dried mud
and had roofs made of straw.
A temple for the Creek Indian gods stood on a hill.
The people built the hill by making a big pile of earth.
The land of the Creek Indians had long, hot summers.
But there were tall, shady trees and wide, cool rivers.

Every Creek girl helped her mother.
She-Likes-Somebody helped her mother do many things.
Sometimes they cleaned strawberries
and cut plums to make fruit bread.
The grandmother wove cloth
out of rabbit hair to make their clothes.
The colors for the cloth
came from berries and plants.
Young Creek girls wore their hair straight down,
but their mothers combed their hair up.

She-Likes-Somebody learned
to work in the cornfields.
She and her mother dug up the ground
with hoes that had stone tips.
The hot sun and rain
made the corn grow fast.
Creek farmers also planted
pumpkins, beans, and squash.

She-Likes-Somebody had a brother named Brave Bear.
He and their father went into the forest to hunt deer
when the family needed meat.
Creek hunters knew how to follow the tracks of animals.
The hunters put deerskins on their backs
so they would look like deer.
The hunters crept very close with their bows and arrows.

Creek girls learned to do many things
by watching their mothers.
She-Likes-Somebody learned to make a clay pot
from long, damp ropes of clay.
She knew how to wind the long pieces,
around and around, into the shape of a bowl.
Then she rubbed the sides smooth.
Before the clay dried, she pressed designs on it
with a wooden paddle. The paddle had designs
carved all over it.

On special days Creek men went to the open field
in the middle of the village.
They dressed up in their jewelry and best clothes,
and they played a game called chunkey.
She-Likes-Somebody and the other people
had fun watching them.
In the game, the men would throw long sticks at a smooth stone
as it rolled across the ground.
The winner was the one who threw the stick
closest to the stone without touching it.

The most important day of the year
came in the middle of summer.
It was the day of the New Fire.
At sunrise on that day,
the priest started a new fire.
It would burn for the whole year.
The priest put ears of new corn into the fire.
Then the people started new fires at home
from the big fire.
They used new dishes and pots,
and everybody wore new clothes.
That was how the Creeks celebrated
the beginning of their new year.

21

A Nootka boy named Center-of-the-Sky lived with his family
in a large wooden house by the sea.
Many families lived together in one house.
There were about ten houses in a village.
Behind the village there was a deep forest with tall trees.
The air was cool and misty in the land of the Nootka,
and rain came almost every day.
In sunny weather, when the day came to an end,
the sun looked like an orange ball sinking into the sea.

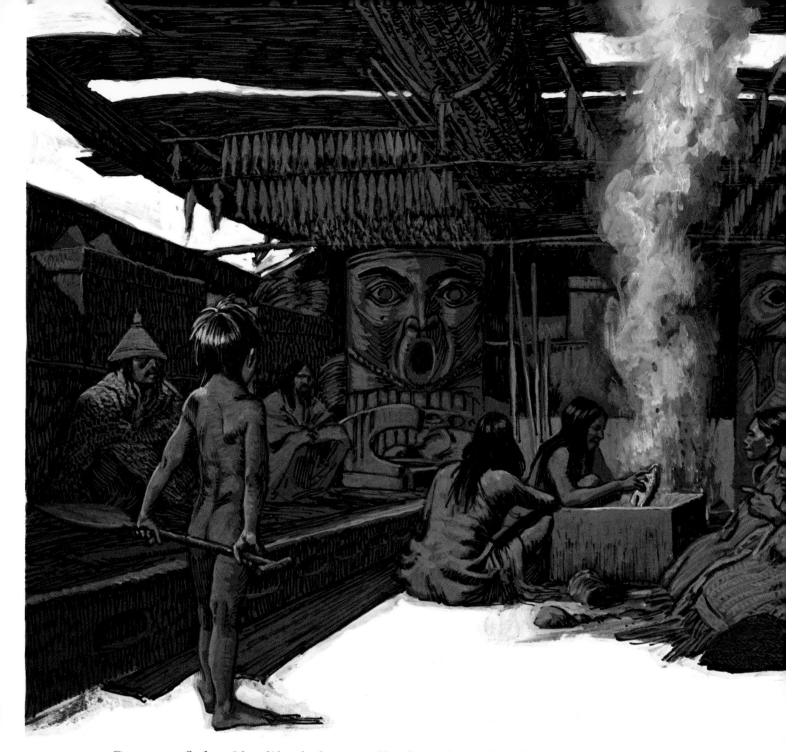

Center-of-the-Sky liked the smell of cooking in the morning.
His mother, grandmother, and aunts cooked at one cooking fire.
They took hot stones from the fire and put them
in a wooden box filled with water.
Soon the stones made the water boil.
Then the women cooked pieces of fish in the bubbling water.
Every Nootka house had large posts that held up the roof.
The Nootka carved faces on the posts so they would not forget
the people who had lived before.

Center-of-the-Sky learned woodcarving from his father.
His father made canoe paddles, boxes,
and many other things.
Center-of-the-Sky watched carefully.
Then he made a little pointed paddle all by himself.

Center-of-the-Sky fished for salmon in
the river. The river made a great noise
as it rushed over rocks.
Center-of-the-Sky would stand very still
on a rock in the middle of the river.
He waited for a fish to swim by. Splash!
Center-of-the-Sky hit a big fat salmon
with a spear called a harpoon.

Center-of-the-Sky would go out on the river with his father
in a canoe. His father had carved the canoe
from a single tree. Center-of-the-Sky learned to paddle
so that one day he could go out to sea to hunt whales.
The Nootka men hunted whales for food and to show
how brave they were. Center-of-the-Sky watched the men
paddle out to sea. He wished that he could go too.

The men hunted whales in the biggest and best canoes.
When the men saw a whale, they paddled close to it.
The chief stood up to stab the whale with his harpoon.
The whale could smash the canoe, so the men paddled away quickly.
The harpoon had floats tied to it. The whale dragged the floats
through the water until it became very tired. Then the men
killed the whale and pulled it to the village where the people waited.

Sometimes a chief gave a big party called a potlatch. At the party
the chief gave away many things—blankets, boxes, and baskets.
One day Center-of-the-Sky felt very proud.
His little, pointed paddle was good enough to give away at a big potlatch.
Like everyone, Center-of-the-Sky ate a lot of fish,
and he danced and sang all the songs he knew.
A fine potlatch with many presents showed how important the chief was.
And the party gave everyone a chance to have a good time.

*Published by* The National Geographic Society
Melvin M. Payne, *President;* Melville Bell Grosvenor, *Editor-in-Chief;*
Gilbert M. Grosvenor, *Editor.*

*Prepared by*
The Special Publications Division
Robert L. Breeden, *Editor*
Donald J. Crump, *Associate Editor*
Philip B. Silcott, *Senior Editor*
Cynthia Russ Ramsay, *Managing Editor*
Marjorie W. Cline, *Research*
*Design and Art Direction*
Joseph A. Taney, *Staff Art Director*
Josephine B. Bolt, *Associate Art Director*
Ursula Perrin, *Staff Designer*
*Production and Printing*
Robert W. Messer, *Production Manager*
George V. White, *Assistant Production Manager*
Raja D. Murshed, Nancy W. Glaser, *Production Assistants*
John R. Metcalfe, *Engraving and Printing*
Mary G. Burns, Jane H. Buxton, Marta Isabel Coons, Suzanne J. Jacobson,
    Joan Perry, Marilyn L. Wilbur, *Staff Assistants*
*Consultants*
Robert V. Duffey, *Educational Consultant*
Dr. Robert L. Stephenson, *University of South Carolina,*
    *Cheyenne Consultant*
Dr. Bennie Keel, *Wright State University, Ohio,*
    *Creek Consultant*
Dr. Philip Drucker, *University of Kentucky,*
    *Nootka Consultant*
Edith K. Chasnov, Lynn Z. Lang, *Reading Specialists*